Flowchart Smart

THE SCIENCE OF OCEANS

Richard and Louise Spilsbury

Gareth Stevens PUBLISHING

Please visit our website, **www.garethstevens.com**.
For a free color catalog of all our high-quality books,
call toll free 1-800-542-2595 or fax 1-877-542-2596.

Cataloging-in-Publication Data

Names: Spilsbury, Richard. | Spilsbury, Louise.
Title: Oceans / Richard and Louise Spilsbury.
Description: New York : Gareth Stevens Publishing, 2020. | Series: Flowchart smart | Includes glossary and index.
Identifiers: ISBN 9781538252284 (pbk.) | ISBN 9781538252291(library bound)
Subjects: LCSH: Ocean--Juvenile literature. | Oceanography--Juvenile literature.
Classification: LCC GC21.5 S65 2020 | DDC 551.46--dc23

First Edition

Published in 2020 by
Gareth Stevens Publishing
111 East 14th Street, Suite 349
New York, NY 10003

Produced for Gareth Stevens by Calcium
Editors: Sarah Eason and Harriet McGregor
Designer: Emma DeBanks
Picture researcher: Rachel Blount

Picture credits: Cover: Shutterstock: Denk Creative (br), Shanesabin (c); Inside: Shutterstock: Kondratuk Aleksei: pp. 20-21; Potapov Alexander: pp. 24-25; Aloneontheroad: pp. 12-13; Barbol: p. 14b; Joe Belanger: pp. 1, 26-27; Willyam Bradberry: pp. 34-35; Brian S: p. 45t; Ethan Daniels: p. 13r; Frantisekhojdysz: p. 5t; Gilkop: pp. 30-31; Leonardo Gonzalez: p. 31t; HappyPictures: pp. 16-17; Andrea Izzotti: p. 21t; Krofoto: pp. 40-41; Ingus Kruklitis: pp. 44-45; Melvin Lee: p. 41t; Anastasia Lembrik: pp. 42-43; Mimadeo: pp. 6-7; NaniP: pp. 28-29; Miriam Newitt: p. 6bl; Ondrej Prosicky: p. 29t; Rhoeo: pp. 32-33; Ian D M Robertson: p. 19t; Damian Ryszawy: p. 35t; Nicram Sabod: pp. 36-37; Siloto: p. 38r; Studiostoks: p. 11; Superjoseph: pp. 4-5, 22-23; Supriya07: p. 39l; Dai Mar Tamarack: p. 27t; Vojce: pp. 9t, 37t; Wildestanimal: p. 23r; Zebra0209: pp. 18-19; Wikimedia Commons: NASA image courtesy Jeff Schmaltz, MODIS Land Rapid Response Team at NASA GSFC: pp. 14-15; NOAA Ocean Explorer: pp. 8-9.

Printed in the United States of America

CPSIA compliance information: Batch #CW20GS: For further information contact Gareth Stevens, New York, New York at 1-800-542-2595.

Contents

Chapter 1

What Are Oceans?

The ocean **ecosystem** is Earth's biggest ecosystem. The world's oceans cover more than three-quarters of our planet's surface. From the shallow waters where we paddle at the shore to the dark, hidden depths in the middle of an ocean, this ecosystem is buzzing with life and activity.

An ecosystem is made up of all of the things that **interact** with one another in an area. It includes living things such as plants and animals, and nonliving things such as the weather, sunlight, and soil. The ocean ecosystem includes everything in the oceans, from the tiniest nonliving pebble to the world's largest living structure—the Great Barrier Reef.

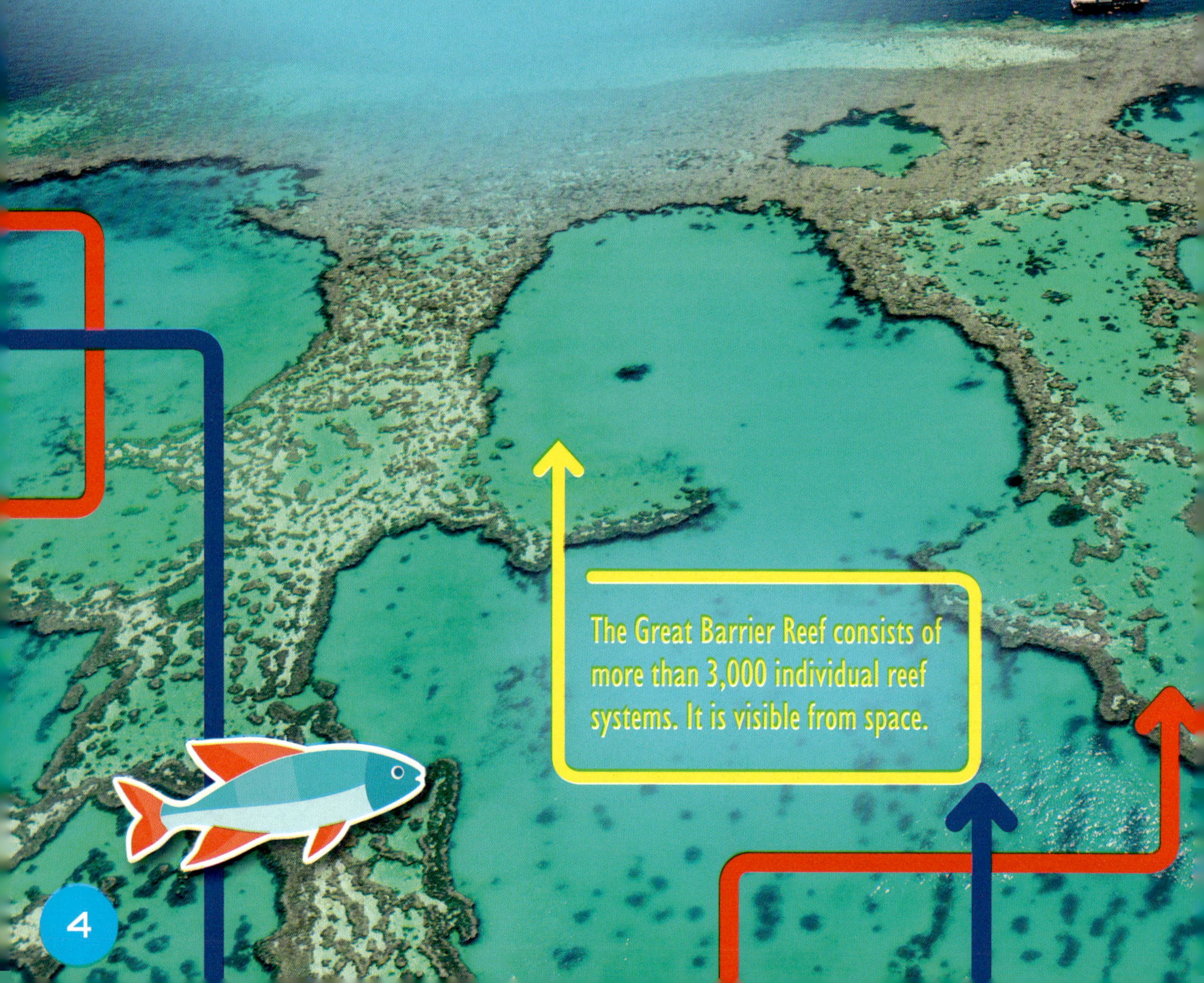

The Great Barrier Reef consists of more than 3,000 individual reef systems. It is visible from space.

Two of the most significant nonliving features of an ocean ecosystem are its salt water and its **oxygen** levels. Most living things cannot drink salty seawater. If they do so, the salt content causes them to dry out and eventually die. Oxygen is a gas that makes up around 21 percent of Earth's **atmosphere**. Most living things need oxygen to survive. In oceans, the oxygen gas is **dissolved** in the water. The lungs of land animals cannot breathe oxygen from water.

When humans explore the amazing world beneath the oceans, they take a tank of oxygen with them so they can breathe underwater.

Get Smart!

Earth has five different oceans: the Atlantic, Arctic, Indian, Pacific, and Southern. However, all the oceans are joined and water flows between them. The oceans are mostly divided up by the seven **continents**, except for the Southern Ocean, which mainly runs into other oceans.

Ocean Features

Two important nonliving features of ocean ecosystems are the tides and waves. Winds across the water's surface whip up high waves that can be very powerful. Tides cause sea levels around the world to rise and fall.

Along the coastlines fringing the oceans, the water slowly rises up until, at high tide, beaches and shores are covered in water. The water slowly falls back again until, at low tide, beaches and shores and all the living things on them are exposed to the wind, hot sun, or cold air. **Mollusks**, such as limpets, have hard shells that keep the sun and wind from drying them out at low tide. At high tide, limpets move very slowly across rocks and eat the **algae** growing on them.

When limpets are exposed to the air, they clamp down onto the rock in order to protect themselves from **predators**.

Waves on the ocean's surface are usually caused by wind, and large waves can travel long distances. Waves come in all shapes and sizes. The smallest waves are smaller than 1 foot (30 cm) high and are called ripples. In contrast, when big waves crash onshore, they can shift huge areas of sand and carve out rocky coastlines. They can even drop boulders as big as cars above the tide line.

The size and power of a wave are influenced by how strong the wind is, how long it has been blowing, and how far the wave has traveled across the ocean.

Get Smart!

Tides happen because of the moon's **gravity**, which pulls on Earth's oceans. Earth is spinning all the time. As it spins, the oceans that face the moon are pulled by its gravity. This makes the water rise and causes a high tide. When the oceans do not face the moon, there is no pull on the water, and low tide returns.

Coastlines, coral reefs, frozen oceans, and deep oceans are all very different. The life-forms found in these places vary.

Far from coastlines, some oceans are incredibly deep. The deeper it gets, the darker and colder the water becomes. Only the top layers of the ocean receive enough light for plants to survive. Most **marine** animals crowd into the top 660 feet (200 m). Below this layer, it becomes darker and darker. Most animals living here eat parts of decaying plants and animal waste that fall from above—or each other.

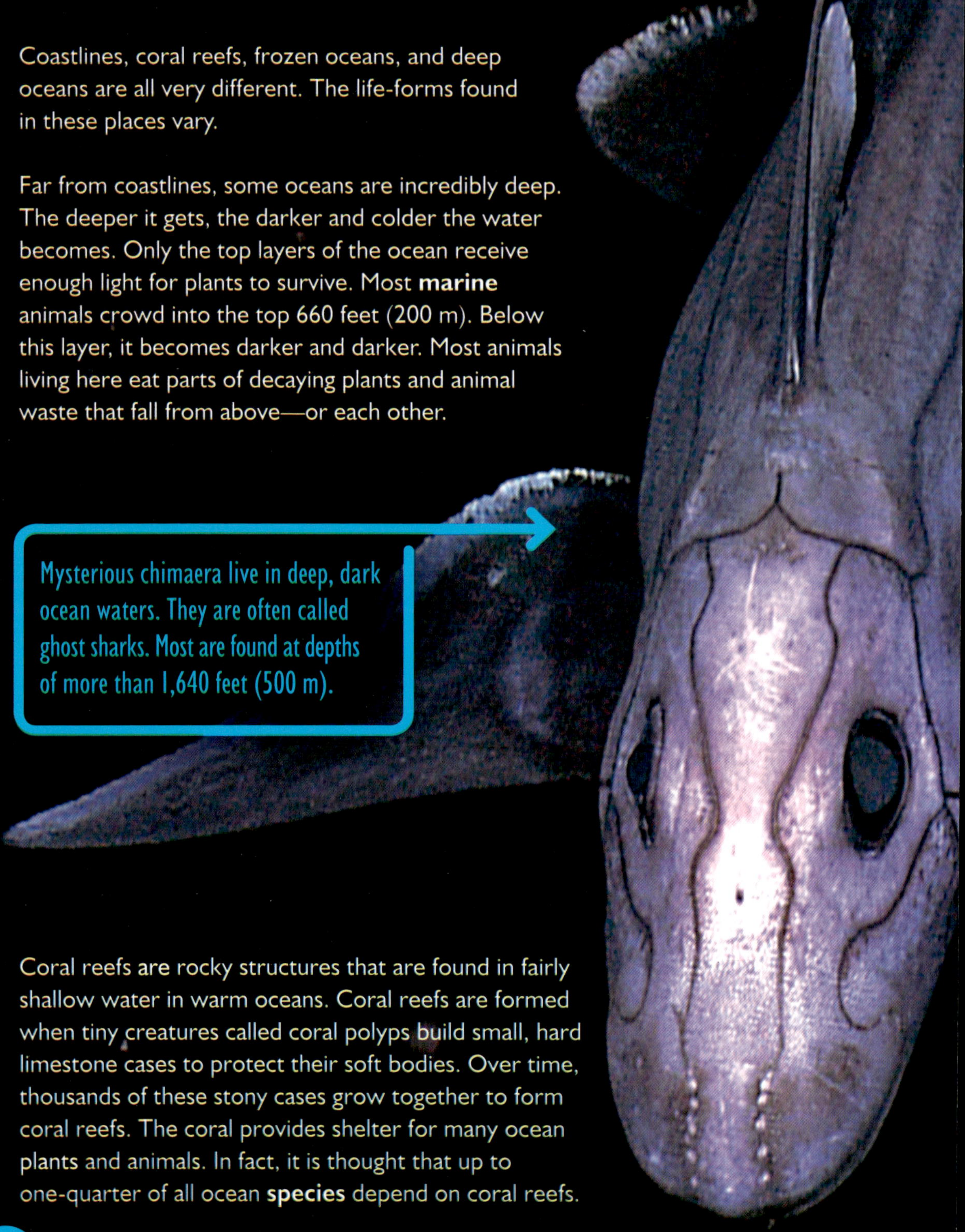

Mysterious chimaera live in deep, dark ocean waters. They are often called ghost sharks. Most are found at depths of more than 1,640 feet (500 m).

Coral reefs are rocky structures that are found in fairly shallow water in warm oceans. Coral reefs are formed when tiny creatures called coral polyps build small, hard limestone cases to protect their soft bodies. Over time, thousands of these stony cases grow together to form coral reefs. The coral provides shelter for many ocean plants and animals. In fact, it is thought that up to one-quarter of all ocean **species** depend on coral reefs.

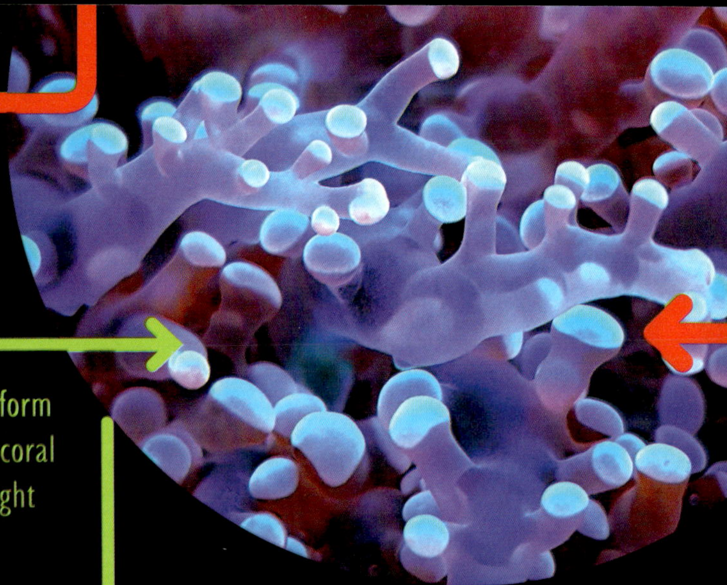

The coral polyps that form branching frogspawn coral can make their own light in deep water.

Get Smart!

Near the **poles**, parts of the Arctic and Antarctic oceans are always frozen. The Arctic Ocean is the smallest, shallowest, and coldest ocean in the world. It contains huge blocks of floating ice, up to 160 miles (260 km) wide. Few animals can survive the freezing temperatures of the Arctic Ocean. Animals that can survive here include polar bears and bearded seals. They have waterproof fur and a layer of fat, called blubber, that keeps them warm.

Get flowchart smart!

How Tides Work

Let's take a look at how Earth's tides are caused.

Tides happen because of the moon's gravity. Gravity is a natural pulling force.

Earth continues to spin.

The place where there was a high tide no longer faces the moon. A low tide takes place.

Earth spins all the time. As it spins, the moon's gravity pulls at the oceans nearest to it.

The pulling force of the moon's gravity causes the water to rise. This results in a high tide.

Flowchart Smart

Chapter 2

Ocean Plants

Algae are ocean plants. They can range in size from the microscopic to the enormous. Small algae float in the ocean while larger, colorful forms of algae, such as seaweed, are found nearer the coast.

The seaweed we see clinging to the edge of the shore uses structures called holdfasts to secure itself on the rock. This keeps waves from dragging it out to sea. Seaweeds also have leaflike parts called fronds. Fronds bend easily so they are not snapped by the waves and they are often covered with slime so that they do not dry out at low tide. Seaweed fronds often have air-filled bladders to help them float at the water's surface.

Seaweeds often form thick blankets on rocky shores or grow in large groups in shallow water.

Kelp are large, brown algae that grow along coasts around the world, especially in cooler regions. Kelp can grow in fairly deep water because they have stems up to 130 feet (40 m) long to hold their fronds near the surface. They must reach and trap sunlight when the tide is in so that they can make food using the process of **photosynthesis**. Kelp stems are also strong so they can withstand the powerful ocean waves that crash into them.

Giant kelp is the largest seaweed in the world. There is an air-filled compartment at the base of each frond. This acts as a float to help the frond reach the sunlight at the ocean's surface.

Get Smart!

During photosynthesis, seaweed and other types of ocean algae take in water and a gas called carbon dioxide from the seawater. They use the sun's energy to turn these ingredients into sugar. The sugar is stored by the plants, to be used as food. Algae also release oxygen during photosynthesis. Humans breathe in this oxygen. In fact, without algae and other plants, there would be no oxygen, and we could not survive.

Floating Algae

Very few plants live in the deep ocean because plants need light for photosynthesis. Light cannot penetrate far into the water. However, tiny algae float on the waves, far out in the ocean, away from the shore.

The tiny algae that drift along in the water and are carried from place to place by the ocean **currents** are called **phytoplankton**. They are very small, but they come in a variety of shapes. Some phytoplankton are flat and round; others have spines or hairs. Their shapes help them keep afloat on the surface of the oceans so that they can reach and trap the sunlight they need to make food by photosynthesis. Scientists believe that phytoplankton contribute between 50 and 85 percent of the oxygen in Earth's atmosphere. In some places, phytoplankton can be found at depths of 600–900 feet (180–275 m). Light cannot penetrate any deeper than this.

The name phytoplankton comes from the Greek words *phyto* (plant) and *plankton* (made to wander or drift).

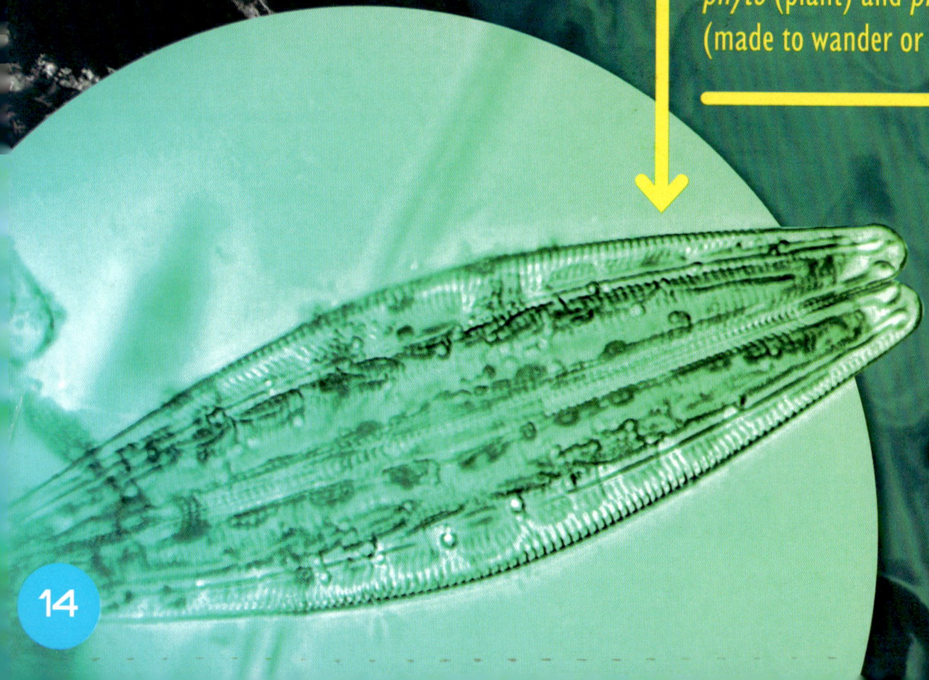

Phytoplankton can be found all over the ocean, but large blooms, or communities, of algae are found in colder waters. Deeper, **nutrient**-filled water rises up toward the cold surface water. The nutrients help the algae grow and multiply. Phytoplankton blooms happen in spring when there is more available light. Some of these blooms of phytoplankton are so huge that they can be seen from space!

Phytoplankton blooms in the ocean may cover hundreds of square miles and are easily visible in satellite images like this.

Get Smart!

Plankton is the name given to the collection of different kinds of tiny phytoplankton, **bacteria**, and animals that float together in the ocean. The tiny creatures in plankton include the larvae of animals such as crabs and jellyfish, and shrimplike animals called copepods. Animal plankton feed on the phytoplankton or on other microscopic animals that form part of the plankton.

Get flowchart smart!

Ocean Algae and Oxygen

Algae such as seaweed trap energy from sunlight in their fronds to help them make their own food by photosynthesis.

Algae take in water and a gas called carbon dioxide from the water around them.

Humans breathe in oxygen. Without algae and other plants, there would be no oxygen, and we would not be able to survive.

They use the sun's energy to turn these ingredients into sugar.

The sugar is stored to be used as food.

During photosynthesis, algae release oxygen into the environment around them.

Flowchart Smart

Chapter 3

Animal Adaptations

Adaptations are special features or body parts that living things develop over time to help them survive in an ecosystem. Ocean animals have some amazing adaptations.

When sea turtles eat animals such as jellyfish, they take in water as well as food. But that water is salty and large quantities of salt are bad for most animals. Some ocean animals get rid of the excess salt by producing very salty urine. However, a sea turtle's body removes salt from the water and empties it from the sea turtle's eyes when the animal is ashore, making it look as though it is crying!

Sharks have gill slits on the sides of their head. When water passes over the gills, very fine blood vessels in the gills absorb oxygen from the ocean.

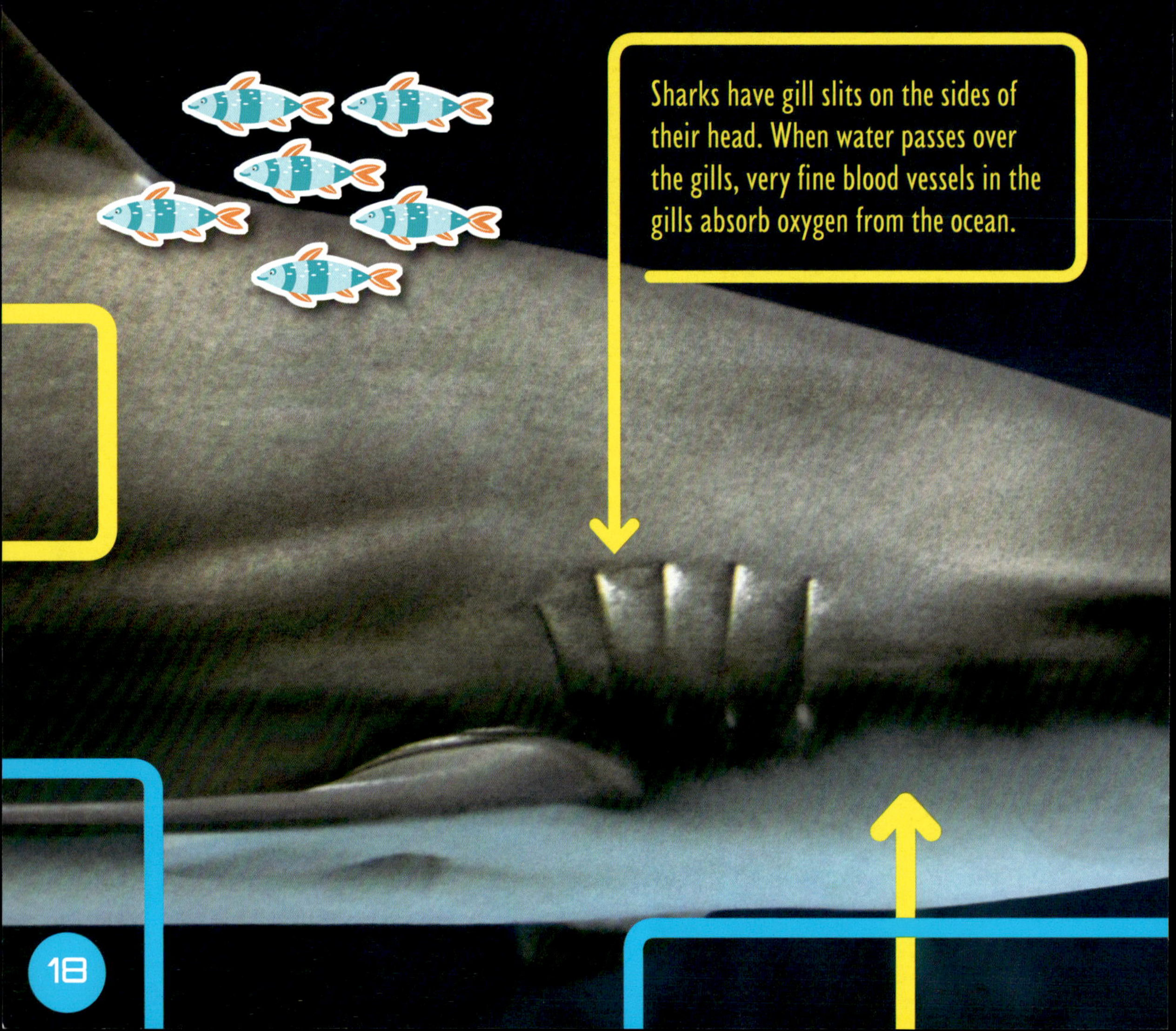

Some animals have unusual adaptations to help them hide from predators. The leafy sea dragon is a seahorse that gets its name from the leaflike parts on its body that look like seaweed. The leafy sea dragon swims so slowly that predators cannot spot the seahorse among the "seaweed." A flatfish is very flat and thin and its body is covered in brown spots. It lies on the seafloor and is **camouflaged** among sand and pebbles.

This leafy sea dragon is perfectly disguised to blend in with the seaweed and kelp in which it lives.

The porcupine pufferfish does not hide. Instead, when it spots a predator it quickly sucks in a lot of water to inflate its stretchy stomach like a balloon. As the pufferfish becomes bigger, the flat spikes on its body stick out and scare the predator away.

Get Smart!

Fish are adapted to breathe underwater using gills. Some fish gulp water into their mouth and pump it over the gills. Oxygen dissolved in seawater passes into the gills and into the fish's body. Other fish force water past their gills as they swim forward with their mouths open.

On the Move

Ocean waves can be rough and **friction** between the water and an animal's body can slow it down. Ocean animals have developed some surprising adaptations to help them move quickly and efficiently through water.

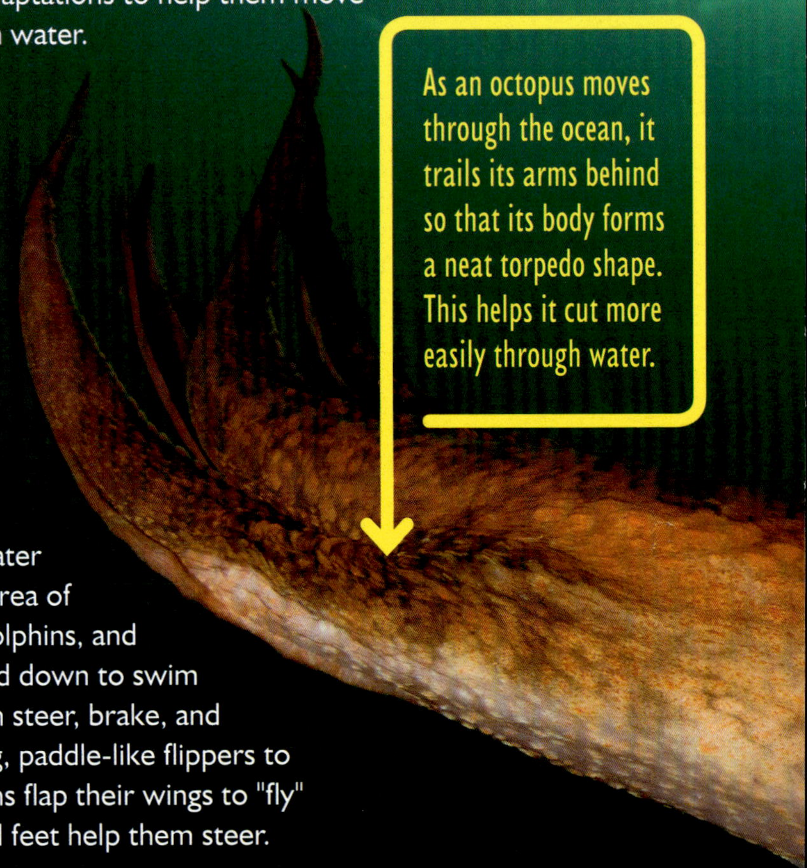

As an octopus moves through the ocean, it trails its arms behind so that its body forms a neat torpedo shape. This helps it cut more easily through water.

Fish, sharks, and many other ocean animals have a long, narrow, **streamlined** body. This shape moves through water more easily by reducing the area of the front of the body. Fish, dolphins, and whales move their tails up and down to swim and dive. Their fins help them steer, brake, and balance. Sea lions have strong, paddle-like flippers to help them move, and penguins flap their wings to "fly" through water. Their webbed feet help them steer.

Some animals move by jet propulsion. Octopuses, squid, and some jellyfish open out the bell-shaped upper part of their body to allow it to fill it with water. Then they squeeze it tight to push the water out backward, pushing their body forward through the water.

Most fish have a gas-filled bag inside their body called a swim bladder. It is located just below their backbone. They fill the swim bladder with air to help them float, and empty the air from the bladder when they want to sink and dive.

Countershading helps the great white shark take its **prey** by surprise.

Get Smart!

The great white shark has a dark back and a lighter-colored underside. This adaptation helps it hunt. When prey animals look up from below, they cannot see the shark because its belly blends in with light shining into the ocean from above. Animals swimming above also do not see the shark because its gray back blends in with the darkness below.

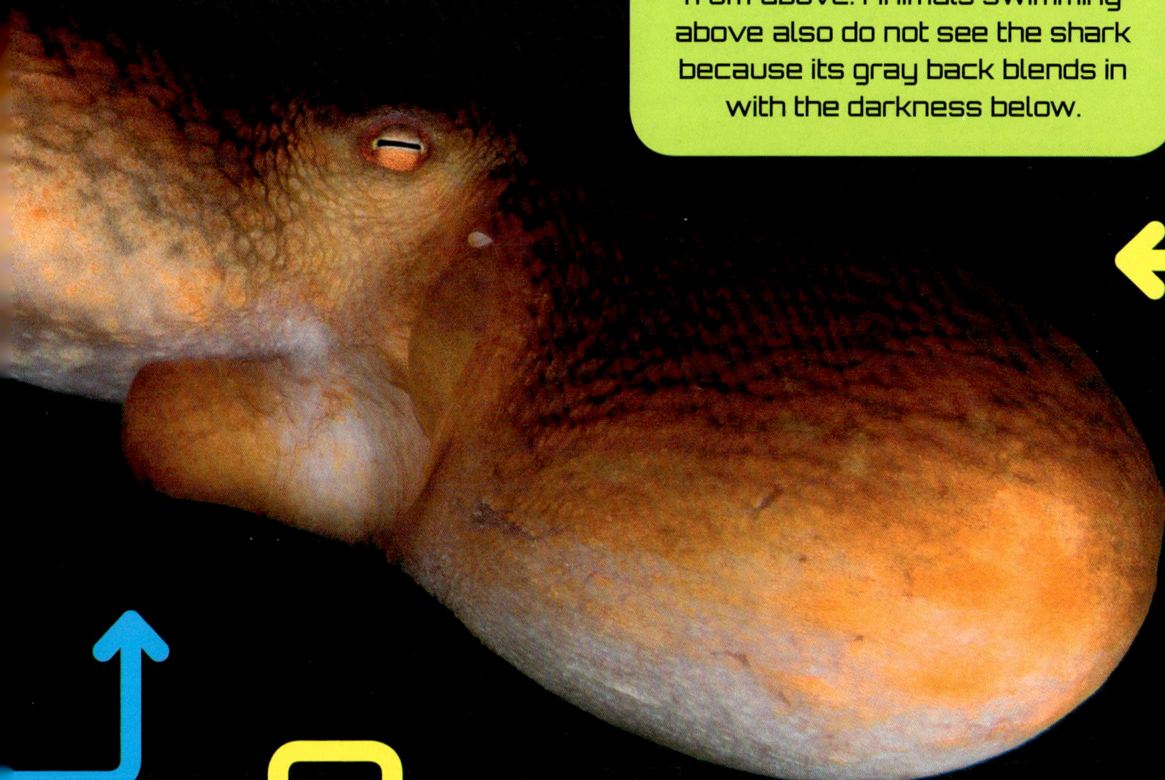

The Deep Dark Ocean

Life in the darkest, deepest depths of the ocean is challenging. It is very cold, pitch black, and the pressure, or pushing force, from the water above is immense. Animals have developed some amazing adaptations to help them survive here.

Some octopuses, squid, and some bizarre-looking fish have adapted to make their own light. Parts called **photophores** on their body contain bacteria that can produce the light. The glowing sucker octopus has a number of photophores on each of its eight arms. Some glow and others twinkle for up to five minutes at a time. Scientists think the light flashes could be used for defense, to attract a mate, or to lure in tiny animals for lunch. Anglerfish have a photophore dangling near their mouth that they use to attract and catch prey.

This deep-ocean fish uses its lure to bring prey close to its very large mouth and sharp, fang-like teeth.

Dolphins find prey in deep, dark ocean waters using sounds instead of sight. First they produce short bursts of noises that sound like clicks to humans. When the sounds hit an animal such as a fish, echoes reflect, or bounce, back to the dolphin. By figuring out where the echoes come from and how long it takes for them to return, the dolphin can locate the fish. This method of locating objects by reflected sound is called echolocation.

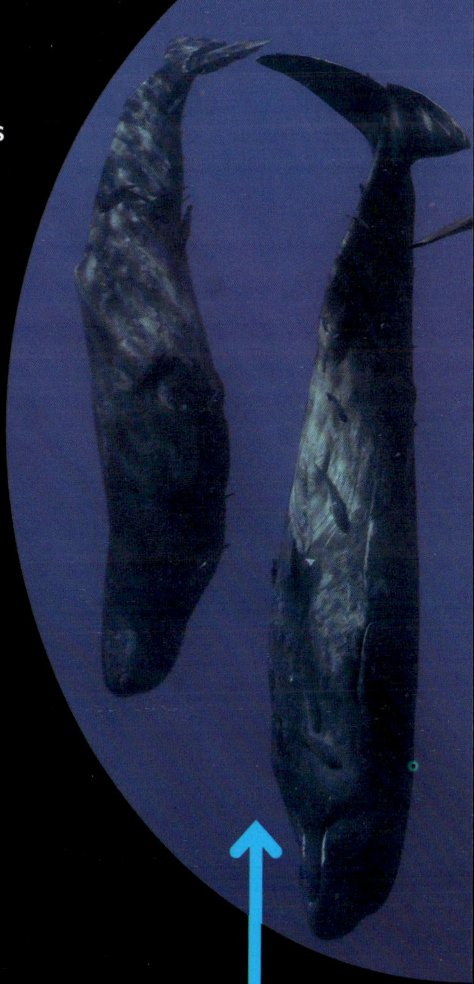

Get Smart!

Sperm whales dive down up to 1.2 miles (2 km) beneath the water's surface while hunting squid, rays, and sharks. An average dive lasts about one hour. The clicks they make to find prey using echolocation are the loudest sounds created by any animal.

Sperm whales use clicks to communicate with one another.

Get flowchart smart!

How Echolocation Works

Discover how dolphins use echolocation to find their food.

A dolphin searches for fish to eat in deep, dark ocean waters.

The dolphin darts forward and snatches its prey.

The dolphin produces short bursts of noises that sound like clicks.

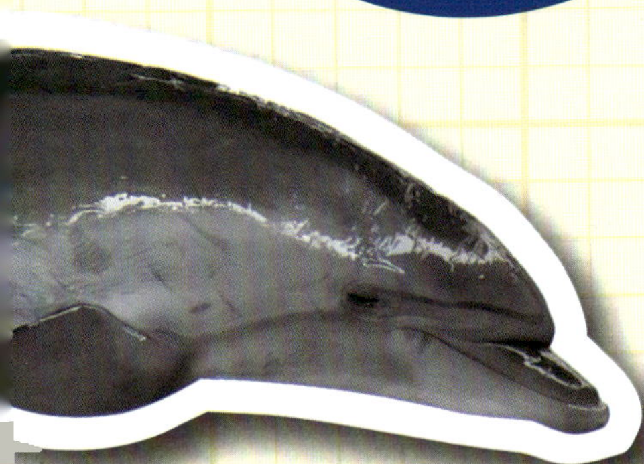

When the sounds hit an animal, such as a fish, the sound reflects, or bounces, back to the dolphin.

By figuring out where the echoes come from and how long it takes for them to return, the dolphin can locate the fish.

Flowchart Smart

Chapter 4

Food Chains

All living things in an ecosystem need food to give them energy to grow, move, hunt, and survive. We can use a food chain to show how energy flows from one living thing to another when it is eaten.

Producers are living things that produce their own food inside their bodies. Ocean producers include phytoplankton and seaweed. Animals that eat producers and one another are called consumers. At the seashore, some animals with shells, such as limpets, use their strong rasping tongues to scrape up small pieces of seaweed. When the tide comes in, barnacles open their shells and wave feathery body parts in the water to catch phytoplankton floating by.

There are more than 1,400 species of barnacle. The feathery, leglike parts are called cirri. They filter, or sift, food from the water.

Sea otters eat their food at the surface of the water. They float on their backs and use their stomach as a table.

Animals such as crabs, lobsters, and most fish eat the algae eaters. A crab's crushing claws can break the shells of mussels and limpets. A starfish can force open a mussel's shell using suction pads on the underside of its body. Then it slides its stomach inside the mussel's shell and dissolves the creature while it is still alive. Starfish themselves are eaten by fish, sea turtles, crabs, otters, and seabirds.

Sea urchins have a hard, beaklike part on the underside of their body, which they use to grind up pieces of kelp. They have spiky shells to deter predators. Unfortunately, the shells do not deter sea otters. When a sea otter catches a sea urchin, it quickly spins the prey in its paws to snap off the prickly spines. Then it breaks open the shell and licks out the insides. Sea otters can eat so many purple sea urchins that their teeth and bones are stained purple!

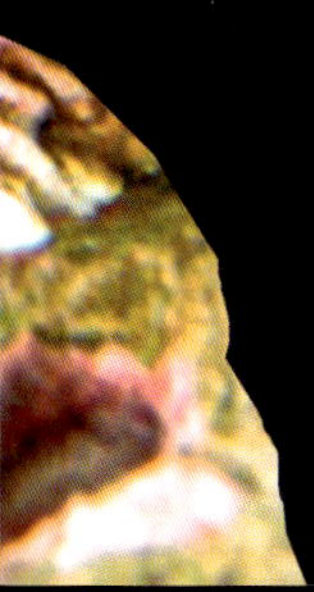

Get Smart!

One animal can be part of several food chains at the same time. For example, a sea otter eats clams, mussels, and crabs. A food web shows how food chains in a particular ecosystem link together.

Frozen Foods

The freezing cold waters of the Arctic and Southern Oceans have their own unique food chains.

Large rafts of ice that float in the Arctic Ocean have algae growing on their undersides. These algae are eaten by small ocean animals such as shrimps. Not all fish could survive the icy waters of the Arctic, but the Arctic cod has a substance in its blood that acts like antifreeze. This substance keeps ice from forming in the cod's blood. Arctic cod feed on shrimps. Ringed seals hunt Arctic cod in the water and return to land to rest. Polar bears hunt seals when they come to the surface to breathe through holes in the floating ice.

Phytoplankton are the producers in Southern Ocean, or Antarctic, food chains. Small, shrimplike animals called krill eat phytoplankton. Krill are ultimately the food for many of the ocean's larger animals. For example, small fish eat krill, and in turn are eaten by penguins. The penguins are eaten by fierce leopard seals, which are fast swimmers and aggressive hunters. They lurk at the edge of the ice, waiting for penguins to dive into the water to feed. Then the seals chase them through the water, catching the birds in their jaws. Leopard seals are strong and powerful. The orca, or killer whale, is their only known predator.

Leopard seals hunt alone and chase prey through water at speeds of up to 25 miles per hour (40 kph).

Polar bears have an incredible sense of smell. They can detect a seal in the water beneath 3 feet (1 m) of thick snow and from a distance of 0.6 mile (almost 1 km).

Get Smart!

The polar bear is an apex, or top, predator in the Arctic Ocean. The orca is the apex predator in the Southern Ocean. These animals are top of their food chains because they eat other animals but are not killed and eaten by any other animals themselves.

Food Chains in the Open Ocean

There is a huge variety of animals in the open ocean. They all need to find enough food to survive. Tiny plantlike organisms called phytoplankton float in the open ocean. They are the basis of almost all open ocean food chains—even giant orcas could not live without them.

Phytoplankton are food for a huge range of small feeders. Countless tiny animals called zooplankton graze on the ocean's phytoplankton. Krill are an abundant and very important type of zooplankton. Smaller carnivores, such as sardines and other fish, eat zooplankton. Larger fish, such as tuna, eat the smaller fish. Finally, the tuna are prey for the largest ocean predators—dolphins, sharks, and whales. These apex predators are usually large, fast, and very good at catching prey.

There are massive fish populations in the open oceans. They include cod, tuna, halibut, haddock, herring, mackerel, and salmon. Many species swim together in large groups, called schools, to protect them from predators. If the fish look alike in size and color, predators can become confused, and find it hard to pick one fish out of the bunch. Larger groups are also better at keeping watch for predators because there are more eyes on the lookout. But even this smart practice cannot outwit one of the greatest ocean hunters—the orca.

Dolphins are found at the very top of some ocean food chains. These sleek ocean swimmers swallow their food whole.

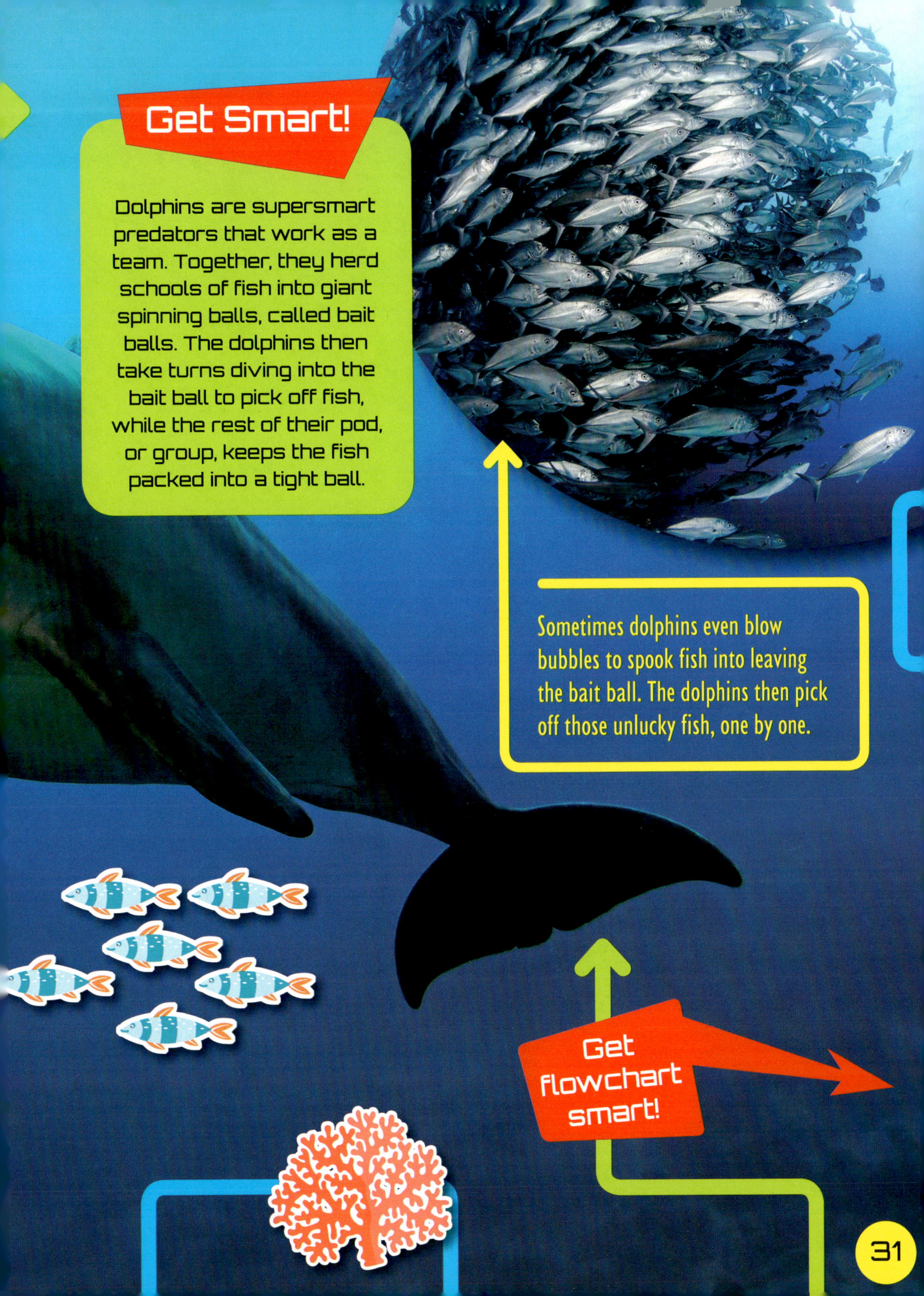

Get Smart!

Dolphins are supersmart predators that work as a team. Together, they herd schools of fish into giant spinning balls, called bait balls. The dolphins then take turns diving into the bait ball to pick off fish, while the rest of their pod, or group, keeps the fish packed into a tight ball.

Sometimes dolphins even blow bubbles to spook fish into leaving the bait ball. The dolphins then pick off those unlucky fish, one by one.

Get flowchart smart!

The Food Chain of an Orca

Let's take a look at this top ocean predator's food chain.

Phytoplankton, a tiny ocean organism, is at the base of this food chain.

Orcas are at the top of this food chain. They hunt and feed on large schools of tuna and mackerel.

Tiny animal organisms called krill feed on phytoplankton.

Krill are then eaten by small fish, such as sardines and herring.

Larger fish, such as tuna and mackerel, feed on the small fish that eat krill.

Chapter 5

Ocean Interactions

The different living and nonliving parts of an ecosystem are interconnected. The living things in an ocean ecosystem rely on the water, sunlight, nutrients, and oxygen dissolved in it to survive. The oxygen and nutrients in the ocean waters come in part from the living things found there.

Decomposers are living things that feed on plant and animal waste that sinks and collects on the ocean floor. Decomposers break down the remains of living things, releasing nutrients from the waste and **recycling** them back into ocean food chains. When a dead dolphin sinks to the ocean floor, hagfish might be the first to feed on its body. Then come snails, worms, shrimp, and finally bacteria.

A current is like a huge river within the ocean, flowing from one place to another. Underwater currents move huge amounts of water from northern oceans to southern oceans, and back again. As well as moving water around the world, currents also move surface waters down and move deeper waters upward. The currents moving upward bring the deep, nutrient-rich water back to the surface for living things nearer the ocean surface to feed on.

Sunlight warms ocean water and creates currents. These currents distribute nutrients and plankton across the oceans.

This fish has washed up on the shore. Decomposers that live on the shore will now feed on it.

Get Smart!

Currents that carry water around the world also affect the temperatures of the oceans. For example, a current called the Great Ocean Conveyor Belt keeps the Atlantic Ocean warmer in winter, which keeps temperatures more comfortable for creatures that live in the ocean.

Sharing Life on a Coral Reef

All the living things in an ecosystem are interconnected in many ways. On a coral reef, there are several examples of these amazing ocean interactions.

Coral polyps are tiny animals that form reefs. They build limestone cases to protect their soft bodies and they also contain tiny algae. The algae and the coral rely on one another to survive. The coral provides the algae with a home and shelter. When the algae make food using energy from sunlight, they pass on some of this food to the coral. In turn, the coral releases waste products that the algae consumes.

As well as providing corals with nutrients, algae are also responsible for the beautiful colors of many stony corals.

Sea anemones give most creatures a nasty sting, but a clown fish is covered in a type of mucus that fools a sea anemone into thinking the fish is just another part of itself. This prevents the clown fish from being stung, which means that it can hide from predators among the anemone tentacles. Clown fish also get to feed on leftovers of fish that the anemone stings and then eats. In return, the clown fish keeps the anemone healthy by eating any damaged tentacles and tiny animals that could damage the anemone.

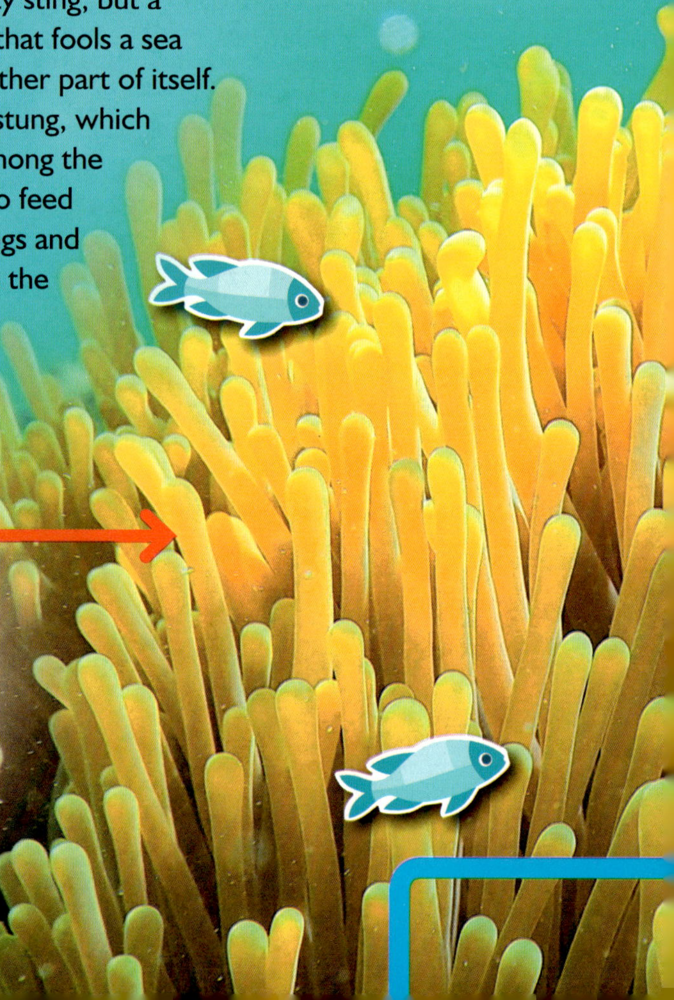

When animals like sea anemones and clown fish make use of one another in a way that helps them both out, scientists call this symbiosis.

Get Smart!

The black stripes between the orange and white markings on a clown fish are different widths on different types of clown fish. Clown fish that live within bigger sea anemones have thicker, darker black stripes. This helps camouflage the clown fish among the shadows of the sea anemone's moving tentacles.

Get flowchart smart!

Clown Fish and Sea Anemone Symbiosis

Let's learn how a clown fish and sea anemone interact and help one another.

A clown fish swims inside a sea anemone's poisonous tentacles.

The clown fish keeps the anemone healthy by eating damaged tentacles and tiny animals that could damage the anemone.

The clown fish is covered in a type of mucus that fools the sea anemone into thinking the fish is just another part of itself. The sea anemone does not sting the fish.

Other fish avoid the stinging sea anemone. The clown fish can hide safely from predators among the anemone's tentacles.

The clown fish feeds on leftovers of fish that the anemone has stung.

Chapter 6

The Future for Ocean Ecosystems

The ocean ecosystem contains a wonderful variety of wildlife. We rely on oceans for many things, including the oxygen we breathe. However, the ocean ecosystem is under threat because people damage and **pollute** it, putting its health and future at risk.

Millions of people worldwide work in the fishing industry or rely on krill, fish, and shellfish as an important food source. The problem is that people are taking more fish from the ocean than can be replaced. This means that some fish, such as the bluefin tuna, are in danger of dying out altogether.

Ocean turtles often eat plastic bags that they mistake for jellyfish, their favorite food.

Accidentally or deliberately, people dump all sorts of waste in oceans, including fishing nets, plastic bags, dirt, chemicals, and oil. Animals can be injured or killed by trash, perhaps because they become entangled in it or mistake it for prey and eat it. Plastic is one of the worst culprits because plastic floats and takes hundreds of years to decompose.

Climate change is the way in which average world temperatures are increasing more rapidly in modern times than in the past. Oceans absorb a lot of this extra heat and this is threatening ocean food chains. For example, krill cannot reproduce if waters become too warm. If there are fewer krill, this will dramatically affect many ocean food chains. Humans are also affected—they are at the top of many ocean food chains because they eat fish and other types of seafood.

Coral bleaching is a sign that a coral reef is in trouble—it is dying.

Get Smart!

Coral polyps make coral reefs, which provide many fish and other animals with food and shelter. When ocean water becomes too warm, the algae that live within the coral stop being able to make food by photosynthesis. Without food made by the algae, the coral can die. The coral starves and turns white, an effect that is known as coral bleaching.

Get flowchart smart!

Climate Change and Coral Reefs

Discover how climate change is affecting our oceans and their coral reefs.

Climate change is making Earth warmer.

Oceans absorb a lot of this excess heat.

The many fish and other animals that live on the reef lose their homes and their source of food.

When ocean waters become too warm, the algae that live within the coral are no longer able to make food by photosynthesis.

Without food made by the algae, the coral can die.

The coral starves and turns white, an effect that is known as coral bleaching.

Flowchart Smart

Protecting Ocean Ecosystems

People all around the world are working to protect ocean ecosystems. Scientists study oceans to learn how changes affect living things. Governments make laws to stop overfishing and create reserves where wildlife is protected. **Conservation** groups raise money to protect ocean animals. What can you do?

You can help limit the effects of climate change by reducing your fuel and electricity use, for example by cycling instead of traveling by car and by putting on a sweater instead of turning the heat up. If your family eats fish, encourage them to buy seafood that is **sustainable** and ocean friendly. When you visit any coastal town, never leave litter and do not buy souvenirs made from various forms of marine life that might be on sale.

Cycling is fun and reduces the amount of gasoline we use, which can help slow down climate change.

Help solve the plastic problem by carrying a reusable drink bottle, taking lunch in a reusable container, and carrying groceries in a reusable cloth bag instead of a plastic bag. Use metal straws instead of plastic because these can be washed and used again, and choose glitter for your art projects that does not contain the tiny bits of plastic that are so bad for the oceans. The oceans are a vital part of our planet's ecosystems. We should do all we can to help them have a healthy future.

Volunteering for a beach cleanup can be a rewarding and useful way of helping ocean wildlife.

Get Smart!

While it is best to try to find alternatives to plastic products or only buy reusable plastic items, it is possible to recycle some plastic. Plastic bottles can be recycled into fleece jackets, kayaks, and many other products. Alternatively, many people choose to buy glass bottles over plastic. Plastic is often only recycled once, but glass can be recycled over and over again. The best thing we can do to protect the planet from plastic is to consume less and reuse more.

Glossary

adaptations Changes to suit a new situation.

algae Plantlike living things found in damp places.

atmosphere The blanket of gases that surrounds Earth.

bacteria Tiny living things that can help decompose waste.

camouflaged Blended in with the surroundings.

climate change A change in the pattern of the world's weather caused by Earth's atmosphere getting warmer.

conservation The act of guarding, protecting, or preserving something.

continents The seven large masses of land on the planet: Asia, Africa, North America, South America, Europe, Australia, and Antarctica.

currents Movements of large areas of water or wind in a particular direction.

dissolved When a solid has broken down and seems to have disappeared into a liquid such as water.

ecosystem The living and nonliving things that interact with each other in a place.

friction The force that slows or stops things as they move against one another.

gravity A pulling force.

interact To act in such a way as to have an effect on one another.

marine Relating to the oceans.

mollusks Animals with a soft body covered by a shell.

nutrient A substance that living things need to survive and grow.

oxygen A gas found in air and water that animals need to survive.

photophores Parts of an animal's body that can produce light.

photosynthesis The process by which green plants make sugary food using the energy in sunlight.

phytoplankton Microscopic marine plants.

plankton Microscopic plants and animals that float in oceans and seas.

poles The two points at opposite ends of Earth, the North Pole and South Pole.

pollute To put something into water, air, or land that damages it or makes it harmful to living things.

predators Animals that catch and eat other animals.

prey An animal hunted and eaten by another animal.

recycling Converting waste into something new.

species A type of animal.

streamlined A long, thin shape that moves well through water or air.

sustainable Causing little or no damage to the environment and therefore able to continue for a long time.

For More Information

Books

Boothroyd, Jennifer. *Let's Visit the Ocean* (Lightning Bolt Books Biome Explorers). Minneapolis, MN: Lerner Classroom, 2016.

MacCarald, Clara. *Exploring Ocean Depths* (Science for the Future). Mendota Heights, MN: North Star Editions, 2019.

Wilsdon, Christina. *Ultimate Oceanpedia*. Washington, DC: National Geographic Children's Books, 2016.

Yasuda, Anita. *Oceans and Seas!* (Explore Your World). White River Junction, VT: Nomad Press, 2018.

Websites

Find out more about the ocean and how climate affects it at:
https://climatekids.nasa.gov/menu/ocean

Read all about the oceans' layers at:
http://kids.nceas.ucsb.edu/biomes/marine.html

Visit this Kids' National Geographic site for fascinating oceans facts:
www.natgeokids.com/uk/discover/geography/general-geography/ocean-facts

Explore more ocean life at:
https://ocean.si.edu/ocean-life

Index